D1470473

Hello, America!

Washington Monument

by Katherine Rawson

Bullfrog Books

Ideas for Parents and Teachers

Bullfrog Books let children practice reading informational text at the earliest reading levels. Repetition, familiar words, and photo labels support early readers.

Before Reading

- Discuss the cover photo. What does it tell them?

- Look at the picture glossary together. Read and discuss the words.

Read the Book

- "Walk" through the book and look at the photos. Let the child ask questions. Point out the photo labels.

- Read the book to the child, or have him or her read independently.

After Reading

- Prompt the child to think more. Ask: What do you know about George Washington? What more would you like to learn about him?

Bullfrog Books are published by Jump!
5357 Penn Avenue South
Minneapolis, MN 55419
www.jumplibrary.com

Library of Congress Cataloging-in-Publication Data

Names: Rawson, Katherine, author.
Title: Washington Monument / by Katherine Rawson.
Description: Minneapolis, MN: Jump!, Inc., 2018.
Series: Hello, America! | "Bullfrog Books."
Includes index.
Identifiers: LCCN 2017027407 (print)
LCCN 2017027863 (ebook)
ISBN 9781624966637 (e-book)
ISBN 9781620318744 (hard cover: alk. paper)
Subjects: LCSH: Washington Monument (Washington, D.C.)—Juvenile literature.
Washington (D.C.)—Buildings, structures, etc. Juvenile literature.
Classification: LCC F203.4.W3 (ebook)
LCC F203.4.W3 R39 2018 (print) | DDC 975.3—dc23
LC record available at https://lccn.loc.gov/2017027407

Editor: Kirsten Chang
Book Designer: Molly Ballanger
Photo Researchers: Molly Ballanger & Kirsten Chang

Photo Credits: AlbertPego/iStock, cover; aphotostory/Shutterstock, 1; Found Image Holdings Inc/Contributor/Getty, 3; Nanette Grebe/Shutterstock, 4 (foreground); Kamira/Shutterstock, 4 (background), 5, 23tl; SuperStock/SuperStock, 6–7; Everett Collection/Alamy, 8–9; Sean Pavone/Shutterstock, 10–11, 23br; National Archives/Handout/Getty, 12, 23tr; Chronicle/Alamy, 13; 4kclips/Shutterstock, 14–15, 23bl; Jorge Salcedo/Shutterstock, 16–17, 24; Interior Department/Alamy, 18; Geoff Renner/robertharding/Getty, 19; MARIIA KONISHEVSKA/Shutterstock, 20–21 (foreground); fstockfoto/iStock, 20–21 (background); holbox/Shutterstock, 22.

Printed in the United States of America at Corporate Graphics in North Mankato, Minnesota.

Table of Contents

A Strong Man

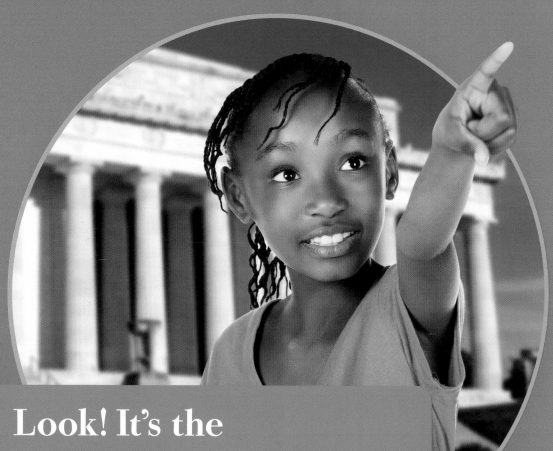

Look! It's the Washington Monument.

It is for
George Washington.

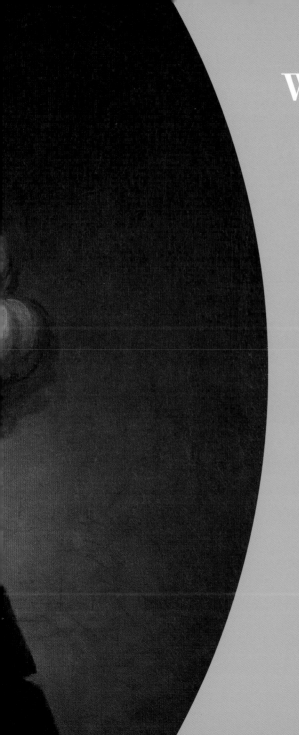

Who was he?

Our first president.

He was a strong leader.

He is called the father of our country.

Washington, D.C.

This building honors him.

It is the tallest structure in Washington, D.C.

It was built in 1884.

It was the tallest
building in the world.

See the top?

It is a pyramid.

Look at all the flags.

There are 50.

One for each state.

Let's go in.

We can go
to the top.

Look out.

We see the city.

We can see far.

We were up there!

A Tall Monument

height
The Washington Monument is 555 feet (169 meters) tall. That is almost twice as tall as the Statue of Liberty!

windows
Small windows at the top of the monument allow visitors to see out. On a clear day, you can see for 30 miles (48 kilometers).

flags
There are 50 flags circling the monument, one for each state in the United States.

stones
The monument is made of more than 36,000 marble stones.

Picture Glossary

monument
Something built
to remember a
person or event.

structure
Something that
is built by putting
pieces together.

pyramid
A shape with
four sides that
meet in a point
at the top.

Washington, D.C.
The capital of
the United States.
It is named after
George Washington.

Index

To Learn More

Learning more is as easy as 1, 2, 3.

1) Go to www.factsurfer.com

2) Enter "WashingtonMonument" into the search box.

3) Click the "Surf" button to see a list of websites.

With factsurfer.com, finding more information is just a click away.